THE BEST OF
THE DEWSWEEPERS:
LESSONS FROM THE LEGENDS

BY TONY RUGGIERO

WITH MATTHEW RUDY

Printed in the United States of America

First Printing, 2015

ISBN-13: 978-1519740816
ISBN-10: 1519740816

Tony Ruggiero
Director of Instruction
CC of Mobile
258 Jackson Blvd
Mobile, AL 36609
Dewsweepersgolf.com

Photographs by Tad Denson

Designed by Tim Oliver (timothypoliver.com)

To Donald Ruggiero and Pasquale Ruggeri,
who started me on this golf journey 38 years ago.

To Mark Wood and Wayne Flint,
who made me want to be better than good.

And to my daughter Abby,
who will always be my pride and joy.

CONTENTS

FOREWORD / BY SMYLIE KAUFMAN

PGA TOUR WINNER

When you play competitive golf, there are plenty of teachers who will tell you what you want to hear. And on video, your swing might even look pretty—which makes it tempting to listen and feel good when somebody is complimenting you about your game.

But if you want to get better, you need somebody you can trust to tell you the truth—the things you're doing well and the things you need to improve—and to give you a plan to make that happen.

I can remember the first time Tony and I worked together, in 2013, when I was still playing at LSU. Our first lesson was at Sunkist Country Club, in Biloxi. From the first part of the first lesson, he was positive but direct, and ready to get going to where I wanted to be as a player. Leaving the practice tee that day, I knew the simple things he gave me where just what I needed. My swing looked good, but I had some fundamentals— grip, posture—that I needed to clean up.

Instead of chasing down a bunch of things that aren't going to help me in the long run, Tony and I have been able to narrow our work down to just a few things on a checklist—just like you're going to hear about in the first chapter. If I have a week when I'm not playing as well, I can go down the checklist. Is it this? Or is it that? It might take a week or two to get back in the swing, but I never get too far off, and I start playing well again.

The best example of this came the last two weeks of the Web.com season. Tony and I worked on two basic things to help me feel comfortable, and get my upper body in a better position with the longer clubs. It immediately paid big dividends when I got out to the PGA Tour. The stakes were higher, but I was comfortable, and I was fortunate enough to win my second start as a member of the PGA Tour, at the Shriners Hospital for Children Open in Las Vegas.

If you spend any time with Tony on the practice tee or listening on the radio, you know that he's an entertaining guy. For me, he's both a golf coach and a life coach. He keeps it loose—we talk about golf swing, football, music, you name it—but he gives you what you need to get better.

I came to Tony with a pretty good swing, but now I feel like I have a swing that's going to be solid day in and day out—and I know how to identify problems when they come up.

Whether you're a 20-handicapper or somebody who wants to get onto the PGA Tour, I think you'll get the same thing from this book—the awareness of how to identify and focus on the right fundamentals, and the tools to make positive changes right away.

FOREWORD / BY LEE WILLIAMS

PGA TOUR PLAYER

When you get out to the PGA Tour, you can pretty much have your choice of instructors. You can pick technical guys who spend lots of time looking at TrackMan, old-school guys who rely on their eye, or guys that specialize in just the short game.

I'm not knocking any of those other teachers, but I can tell you that Tony offers something pretty uncommon. He's able to give you things that work throughout your whole game—from full swing to putting. You aren't thinking about one thing while you hit the driver and something totally different when you hit short irons. He understands the swing, and he gives you simple, clear advice on how to improve.

And beyond that, Tony is truly a coach. That's another thing that's pretty rare. Anybody can look at numbers on a screen. Tony knows the numbers, but he shows you how to be a player.

That idea is even more important for a regular player than it is for guys playing for a living. If you're a bogey golfer, chances are you don't have a clear idea of what you need to do to get better. Getting slammed with a bunch of technical information and TrackMan data isn't going to make you better. Would you rather know if you're swinging down on it two degrees, or get something that will help you correct your problems without getting cluttered by stuff that doesn't matter?

I enjoy my work with Tony because he's so consistent with his message, and he's able to narrow it down to the truly important things I need to do to get better. Then we get to work, and I don't get too many surprises. That really lets me focus.

Tony is a great teacher, and a great guy—something I think you'll see as you go through this book. He's really funny, and he doesn't take himself too seriously. He's also one of the easiest guys in the world to pick on, because he's such an easy target.

But all joking aside, I've been to some of the top instructors in the world, and Tony is as good if not better than anybody I've ever worked with.

I'm looking forward to seeing what we can accomplish next.

FOREWORD / BY ROBBY SHELTON

ALL-AMERICAN AT THE UNIVERSITY OF ALABAMA

The first time I heard about Tony Ruggiero, I was 12 or 13 years old, and I really didn't like the way my swing looked. I saw what he was doing with Bobby Wyatt, and I wanted to see if he could help me.

From the first time we ever got together, I knew it was going to be a long-term thing. We just clicked. Tony knows the swing, but more importantly, he knows how to give you just the right amount of information at just the right time.

If I'm getting ready for a tournament, he's not piling on a bunch of information that can mess up your mind. He gives me the one simple thing I need to go out and play well. But if there's work to be done during an open stretch, he's there with you for every ball, helping you figure it out.

But if you really want to know about Tony, just watch him work at one of his junior camps. It's amazing to see him with kids and beginners. He's laid back and so easy to be around, and he makes everybody want to play the game. His approach with a bogey golfer or young kid isn't much different than it is with somebody trying to play with a living—he's still delivering information in a way the player in front of him can handle it.

He's old school in the best way. He doesn't need a screen to tell you what's going on, but he's comfortable with all of the new technology and will use it if it will help a player.

I can tell you that working with Tony, he has my swing to where I love it. That's where confidence comes from, and I'm looking forward to getting even better with his help.

I'm glad you're getting the same chance here in *Lessons from the Legends*.

INTRODUCTION

Nobody does it alone.

Whether you've listened to me talk to some of the most accomplished teachers in the game on The Dewsweepers, my instruction show on the PGA Tour Radio and SiriusXM radio, or just followed the personal stories of any great player in this game.

We all have mentors and teachers—people who have grown the game both inside us and for the rest of the golf world.

One of the main reasons I started The Dewsweepers—and why I'm writing this book—was to hear more from the teachers who inspired and mentored me, and to share that knowledge with as many people as possible.

I'll be the first one to say that I'm lucky to have learned under some of the best. Mark Wood was my teacher when I was in high school, in Birmingham, Alabama. When I got to college, I took lessons from Wayne Flint. When I was just starting out as an instructor, Wayne and Hank Johnson took me under their wings and helped a guy who was literally down to his last $50 grow into a teacher who has had the chance to change a lot of golfers' lives.

Fifty bucks isn't an exaggeration, either.

Hank and Wayne helped get me my first job, at a semi-private club in Perdido Key, Fla., called The Sportsman Golf Club. I was a cart boy, but I could also teach as much as I wanted on the side. I averaged about $8 an hour that first year, and I got my truck repossessed. By the end of the year, I was renting a little cottage off Canal Road in Orange Beach that for a good three months didn't have any electricity. I didn't have enough money to pay the bill.

But I kept working at it. I would drive to Birmingham on some off days and watch Wayne or Hank teach lessons, and tee up balls for their students all day. My teaching got better bit by bit.

I gave a lesson or a tip to a guy named Joe Gilchrist, who owned a popular hangout called the Flora-Bama beach bar, before a scramble one day out at the Sportsman. He loved guys who were chasing the dream, and when he heard my story he gave me a card that would let me get free cheeseburgers. If it weren't for Joe, Jack Robertson, Fred Villamoor, Olivia Coates and a few others, I would have certainly starved and gone thirsty! (To this day, I spend one afternoon at the Flora-Bama every time I go back to the beach. I'll never forget those people who took care of me.)

For more than a year, that's how I ate, until Hank and Wayne had an opening for a golf school they ran in Sandestin, Fla. They asked me to come down and interview for the job, and I borrowed a friend's old Cadillac to make the 50-mile drive over from Perdido Key.

I'll never forget getting that job, and how grateful I was to get my chance to work as an assistant under those two guys. They sat me down and showed me the basics of how to make any player improve—grip, posture, pivot and divot.

I helped them with the school, and I had them teach almost every one of my students while I watched, so I could see what I was getting right and wrong. They were amazing mentors. They always made me look smart and helped the students get better. I learned a powerful lesson very early—that if you keep your students' interests at heart and make them better, even if that means bringing in other teachers, your business will grow.

Mine did, little by little. That first year, I made $52,000 teaching—which seemed like all the money in the world.

A few years later, a local radio guy I knew came to me with an idea. He knew I was teaching a lot of local businesspeople, so he asked if I was interested in doing a one-hour general golf show live every Saturday morning at 7 a.m. I jumped at the chance, and started chatting with callers about Tiger Woods and tour golf and anything else they wanted to talk about.

The Dewsweepers was born.

But one of my students, Ralph Carroll, had a lot experience in the music and radio promotion business, and after hearing the show, he came to a lesson with some constructive criticism.

He told me that the best part of the show was when I talked about golf instruction. "Your gift is teaching," he said. "That's what you should be talking about." He saw The Dewsweepers as something more along the lines of Golf Channel's Academy Live program—interviews with top teachers, and more question-and-answer with listeners about their own swings, not Tiger Woods'.

Ralph couldn't have been more right.

Within a few months, I was talking to two or three of the best teachers in the world every week, and my listening audience grew to the point that The Dewsweepers was syndicated to stations in Jackson, Nashville and Birmingham, among others. Not only was my listening audience growing but I was having conversations with the best teachers in the world every week.

At the start, my only goal was to increase my local profile and learn more about how to help people. Now,

I was on all of the stations in the drive-to market surrounding Sandestin. In 2007, the show got picked up by PGA Tour Radio for SiriusXM, and we're now the longest-running instruction show on the network, and the second-longest running show overall.

With that exposure, I've been able to build relationships with many more teachers—some that you'll read about in the chapters to follow. Bryan Gathright who was longtime assistant of Harvey Penick, Tom Patri and Brady Riggs have become friends because of the show, as has teaching legend Jim McLean—who is still gracious enough to text me back advice when I have a complicated teaching question.

It all started with the show, and working on the radio asking questions every week to these great teachers has made me a much better, more curious teacher. Being exposed to so many different philosophies and approaches has given me the ability to pick and choose what works for me and to broaden my horizons.

Having an open, flexible approach backed by the fundamentals I learned from my mentors has helped me develop a following among some of the best junior and amateur players in the country. I came to the Country Club of Mobile in 2011, largely because of the work I had done with Bobby Wyatt—who became the No. 1-ranked junior player and amateur player in the world and won two national championships at Alabama during our time together.

That grew into work with Robby Shelton, Lee Williams and Smylie Kaufman—who just earned his PGA Tour card for 2016 and notched his first win in just his second start.

The first time I ever went to the U.S. Open as a teacher, with Robby, Sam Love, and Smylie in 2014 at

Pinehurst, I can remember seeing Butch Harmon on the range and being more concerned about what he was doing with his student than I was doing with mine! I didn't feel like I belonged. Now, I've been able to have some big moments of my own, I want to take that next step as a teacher. I want to help develop successful players on the big tour, and celebrate with then when they win Tournaments and Major Championships.

But even if that kind of success comes, some of the "smaller" victories are still the most satisfying. After all, a thoroughbred is always going to be fast—you're just helping him go a bit faster.

One of my junior students was born severely premature, and doctors believed he'd never be able to do anything athletic. Two years ago, he came to me with the goal of playing high school golf. The first time we played nine holes, he tried for two hours before he could get a ball airborne. He must have hit 200 shanks in that hour but he hung in there I kept placing the ball up next to a 2x4 and taught him to turn to his front foot, pitch the ball with out throwing the club head. We have kept at it, and now he's shooting in the 70s regularly and is getting ready to play for a junior college team.

And that's really the message for anybody reading this book.

Every single one of us can get better. And we can all use help from the great teachers and players in this game.

The backbone of *Lessons From the Legends* is just that—a collection of lessons I learned from my conversations on The Dewsweepers. We'll start with legendary teacher Mark Wood, and the notecard process he uses with all of his students. I've adapted the technique for my own teaching, and learning how to summarize all of your important lessons is going to help you get better so much faster.

After Woody, we'll talk about PGA Tour player Lee Williams and his practice techniques, and Golf Magazine Top 100 teacher Brady Riggs on the strategies he uses to help good players break 80 for the first time. Two of my favorite people make up the next two chapters. Two-time Masters champion Ben Crenshaw has always been the master of turning a bogey into a par, and Golf Digest Top 10 teacher Mike Adams has done more to show golf instructors how to use all the tools at their disposal than almost anyone in the game.

Tom Ness has been teaching players how to make the most important move in golf for more than 30 years. In Chapter 6, I'll talk about Tom's lessons on the pivot controlling the swing. Next, I'll share Wayne Flint's advice about the basics, and lastly, I'll talk about how to make a real game improvement plan.

It doesn't matter if you're an aspiring tour player or somebody who just wants to shoot a better score at the club next weekend. The collected wisdom from these teaching and playing greats will help you as much as it's helped me.

I'm looking forward to spending some time with you.

—TONY RUGGIERO / MOBILE, ALA.

1

THE NOTECARD

*"If you can't fit everything the student needs
on a 3x5 notecard, you haven't done your job."*
— Mark Wood

I was a pretty good high school golfer when I moved from Houston to Birmingham in the summer of 1987, thanks to regular help from local club pros. When we got to Alabama, I was exposed for the first time to real teaching when my dad took me over to a local driving range called Linkside.

Linkside positioned itself as a place with terrific instruction—an idea ahead of its time in the middle 1980s. I got my first lesson there with Mark Wood, who was in the middle of building one of the strongest junior programs in the country.

Mark sat me down and made me an offer.

"You can come take as many lessons as you want, and it'll cost you $100," Mark told me. "But the catch is, you have to go out and earn the money yourself."

I had a job as a cart boy at Inverness Country Club right down the road from Linkside. I was eager to earn that $100 and get started.

I just about wore Mark out taking lessons that first summer. I was determined to get better, although I can't vouch for how well I listened sometimes. I can remember one day when Mark dumped an entire barrel of balls at my feet and told me to come get him when I figured out how to hit my driver in the air off the turf! This was back in the days of persimmon, and getting my Toney Penna driver airborne when I was swinging up and out on the ball was no easy task.

Woody is a master at motivating and making a point.

His lessons are ones I carry with me to this day. Not only did the lessons help me make it as a college golfer, but Mark was my first inspiration for wanting to become a golf instructor.

I started my college playing career at St. Mary's, a small university in San Antonio with a up-and-coming golf program. On my first break as a freshman, I came back east and spent some time at my grandparents' house in Lakeland, Fla.—which happened to be close enough to Innisbrook Resort, where Mark had just moved from Birmingham.

Mark's then-fiancee (and now wife) Kathy picked me up from the airport, and I'll never forget spending hours at Mark's place, watching him run VHS tapes of students' swings on the television in his living room and draw on the screen with a dry erase marker.

Flash forward 15 years, and I'm on my way in the golf business as a teacher. Woody and I have always kept in touch, and he's been a regular guest instructor at my junior programs.

The first time he came to speak to one of my groups, he told a story that really connected with everybody in the room. Woody teaches Bo Van Pelt on the PGA Tour, and he said that every time they worked together, they'd finish the lesson by writing out a simple summary of the main points on an index card.

"If you leave a lesson with more than you can write on that little card, you haven't done a good job," he said.

Mark and Bo extended that idea to their work in between seasons, too. Mark would leave Bo with a notecard of three or four main ideas to work on in the offseason, and Bo's job was to concentrate on just those ideas—not anything extra "outside the lines," so to speak.

It's something I do for all of my students now. I'll look at their baseline fundamentals (which you'll read about in the following chapters). From there, I'll figure out which of those are out of whack, and what plan we're going to make to address it.

That becomes the first notecard.

For example, a new student's might say "hip posture at address, wind trunk into the right hip, finish on your front foot." That's it. And when the student looks back on the card later on, at the range, he or she can instantly connect the ideas on the card with the particular things we talked about in the lesson and the feels to match.

I love this idea for a lot of reasons. First, it narrows your focus to a few main points. The golf swing can be complicated, especially if you're trying to fix all of it at once. You're going to improve more quickly and more consistently if you tackle your problems one at a time.

It also gives you a cool way to build a record of your "instruction life." By keeping a collection of those cards indexed by time, you can go back at any point and pick something that might have connected for you in a different, more useful way.

Interestingly enough, I've found that it doesn't matter if I'm working with a junior, a regular club player or somebody playing for a living—everybody has tendencies that stay with them no matter what. Call it golf DNA.

That's why it's so useful to have cards from months and years past, because the chances are really good that you're going to come up against some of the same issues.

Take Smylie Kaufman for an example. During the summer in the weeks following his Web.com tour win, he struggled with his ball-striking. We made a conscious effort to go back to the five things we know he needs to do to play his best golf—posture, ball position and aim, taking the club back connected and with his pivot, staying centered on his backswing pivot and not moving off the ball, swinging the grip on top of the plane coming down, and finish his pivot without hanging back.

It helped him to have another set of eyes verifying what he was doing, but he knew what needed to be done on his own. It's one more way to feel more confident about the work you're putting in and your ability to not only consistently take it to the course, but get it back when things are going sideways.

I believe the real key to constant improvement every day, every practice and every round is to stay committed to your note card. If you stay on that note card, every practice or round will build towards helping you become a better player and at the end of the year you will have improved. And if at the end of the year you're a better player than when you started, you're headed toward the ultimate goal.

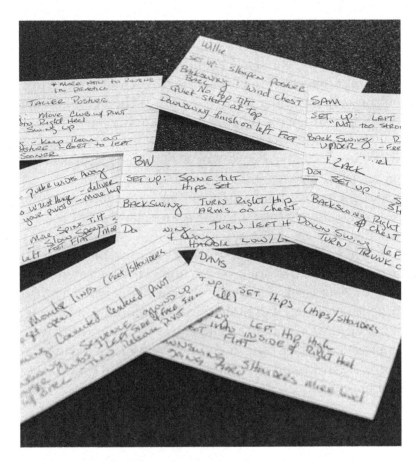

IF YOU LEAVE A LESSON WITH MORE INFORMATION THAN
YOU CAN FIT ON AN INDEX CARD, YOU'RE TRYING TO PROCESS TOO MUCH.
SIMPLIFY TO THREE OR FOUR MAIN POINTS AND WORK ON THOSE.

2

HOW TO PRACTICE

"I want to look back at the end of each year and see that I'm a better player than I was at the start of the year. If I am, then I will get to where I want." — Lee Williams

There might have been a time when a super-talented player could make it out on the to the PGA or LPGA tours on talent alone and not have to put in the practice. But those days are long gone.

If you want to put a tee in the ground for the first time on one of the top professional tours, you need to put an amount of time into your game that most regular people would think was crazy.

The standard obviously isn't as high if you're an amateur trying to improve in between working your regular job and being with your family, but the overall point is still an important one.

You can't expect to go out and play well—and improve—if you don't put in the practice.

Lee Williams is the best kind of student. He has all the talent in the world, and he's the hardest practicer I've ever been around. I met Lee when he was playing for Auburn and working under Hank Johnson—who was a mentor of mine.

Lee had a terrific amateur career, playing on two Walker Cups and earning All-America recognition three times at Auburn. He was the runner-up in the 2003 NCAAs as an individual, and made it to the semifinals of the 2003 U.S. Amateur.

After leaving Auburn and turning pro in 2005, Lee kept in touch through the years. A few years ago, I was heading up to Auburn to work with one of the players on the team and Lee came over from his home in Alexander City, Ala., to have some lunch and talk about the state of his game.

He had tried a few things and gotten off track by doing what so many players do—search and bounce from fix to fix.

Golfers of all skill levels find themselves searching for pieces of information that are going to dramatically change their golf swing and their golf game. I hate to tell you, but there isn't any magic or pixie dust out there.

No one can tell you one simple thing that will turn your 15 handicap into scratch, or make you a PGA Tour winner if you're a struggling mini-tour player.

You can get there, but you need to do with a plan that's tailored to your game. That's what Lee and I did when we sat down for lunch.

Like I said, practice effort has never been a problem for Lee. The goal was to channel all of that energy and determination into productive improvement.

The quickest way to do that is to make sure you're practicing what you mean to be practicing.

A practice station is absolute must no matter what your playing level is. By setting it up with the right reference points, you can look down and be absolutely sure you're set up the way you need to be, aimed where you want to be and starting the ball where you intend to be.

I start every student with the same kind of basic station, and they can adapt if from there if they're looking for some extra or different information.

Begin by stretching some rope tight on the ground on the target line, and secure the ends with tees. Now, you can set up with the ball on or right next to that line and immediately see not only how you're aiming your body and the clubhead in relation to the target, but also where the ball starts after you hit it.

Next, lay a practice stick or a second club on the ground in between your feet, perpendicular to the target line. Set that marker up so that it points to where you want your ball position to be for the given shot you're practicing.

This isn't the time to be mindlessly beating ball after ball. You want to go through your process and make sure you're getting yourself lined up correctly to the guide rope and ball position marker.

What ball position is right for you?

It depends on a few factors, like your predominant shot shape and body makeup, but in general, the driver is even with your left heel (for a right-handed golfer). I start every student the same way: Start with the ball one clubhead width inside your left heel. You always want to hit the ball before the turf, which makes the low point of the swing in front of the ball. On a good swing, the club will intersect with the ground below your lead shoulder. Placing the ball one clubhead inside that shoulder will promote that ball-first contact.

Ball position appears to change as the iron gets longer or short, but what really happens is that the relationship between the ball and the front foot stays the same, but you widen your stance the longer the iron gets. Pay attention to this fundmantal during your practice and your consistency of contact will dramatically improve.

The key distinction between players like Lee and Robby Shelton and average club players is that the tour-level guys go into every practice station working on something on purpose. Lee has his written list of keys with him, and he's doing something intentional with his practice to make some part of his swing better. Every swing is set up so that he can practice hitting good shots.

Compare that to what most players usually do at the range and it's easy to see why tour players get so much more out of all the practicing they do. Most average players hit a few shots, and when one doesn't come off the way they like the start tinkering with a few different things. Maybe they change grips, or they bring the club back a different way. They're experimenting, hoping to find the magic cure for their problem ball flight.

The end result is that when they hit a bad shot they don't know what caused the bad shot and when they hit a good shot they have no clue what caused the good shot either.

I say this to my students all the time: I want you to learn what you need to do to hit your good shot. When you understand what that is, go to the range and work on doing that over and over again instead of concerning yourself about what causes the bad shots.

If you don't have a system in place for doing your improving on purpose and with a plan, you go and try to play with that experimental idea and you can't remember or recreate it on the course, under pressure.

It might feel satisfying to go and buy the biggest bucket at the driving range and work through all of your clubs—messing with your ball position on the driver, changing around a bunch of things you do with your short irons.

But when you don't make an improvement plan and pick a single, simple thing to work on during your range session, you're actually making the process of improvement happen slower—if it even happens at all.

Lee is proving that concept to be true all over again right now, as he comes back from some back troubles that cost him most of the 2015 season. He's incredibly committed to the step-by-step process of improvement, and he's willing to put one foot in front of the other.

It makes me want to go out, put some rope down, and hit a bucket of balls!

One of the most common questions I hear on the radio

show comes from amateurs wanting to know how much time tour players actually spend practicing at a tournament site and during off weeks.

It depends on the player, but I've learned so much on the subject from my friend Dr. Bhrett McCabe, a sport psychologist on the PGA Tour. Doc explains that the best players are the ones most directed and efficient with their practice.

Football teams script out their plays and practices. Golfers would get the same benefit—and tour players do.

Here's what a practice plan looks like for another one of my guys, Web.com player Sam Love:

SUNDAY

Full swing — use rope

FOCUS ENTIRELY ON RIGHT HIP

EVERY CLUB YOU HIT START WITH 5 SHOTS DOING DRILL OF PRE SET HIP

WORK YOUR WAY THROUGH BAG

EVEN OR ODD CLUBS 15 TOTAL SHOTS PER CLUB

When you are done with this your full swing session is over. You're done! Leave the tee!

Putting — address our weakness

MAKE 50 4 FOOTERS IN A ROW

STRAIGHT UP HILL. GO THROUGH ROUTINE EACH TIME.

When you're done practice is over.

MONDAY

After flight

HIT BALLS ON ROPE

FIRST 20 BALLS WORKING ON RIGHT HIP

NEXT 25 BALLS 5 BALLS PER CLUB WORK YOUR WAY THROUGH SET USE PRACTICE STATION WITH ALIGNMENT STICK BETWEEN YOU AND TARGET. MAKE BALL START OVER STICK OR TO LEFT NOT RIGHT AND CURVED RIGHT

CHIP/BUNKER 30 MINS

WALK 9 HOLES

You're done.

TUESDAY

Prior to practice round

HIT BALLS ON ROPE

20 BALLS WORKING ON RIGHT HIP

50 BALLS CHANGING CLUBS BUT USING PRACTICE STATION WITH ALIGNMENT STICK IN BETWEEN BALL AND TARGET

Practice round

After practice round — Putting

50 4 FOOTERS

You're done! No more.

WEDNESDAY

Putting

50 4 FOOTERS

Chipping / pitching / bunker — 1 hour

PITCH BALLS 20-30-40-50-60 YARDS. USE LASER KNOW DISTANCES YOU ARE PITCHING EVERY SHOT DON'T JUST HIT PITCH SHOTS. GET SOMETHING OUT OF EVERY SHOT

Full swing — use rope

25 BALLS ON ROPE FIRST 5 WITH HIP PRESET AT ADDRESS 60 BALLS CHANGING CLUBS AND TARGETS EVERY SHOT FOCUSED ON HITTING A SHOT AT THE TARGET

You're done.

THURSDAY

Pre round

WARM UP AS USUAL

LAST 4 SHOTS YOU HIT SCRIPT FIRST TWO HOLES HIT YOUR FIRST DRIVE ON ONE AND THE SECOND SHOT ETC FOR HOLES 1 AND 2.

Do this twice before you finish then you are ready to play.

OUR GOAL

1) Have you more rested Thursday
2) Practice with a plan and purpose which keeps you

focused on what we want you to do in your golf swing not guess try or wonder about things during the week. We aren't going to change what we are trying to do based on one shot or day or week. This is a plan!

A specific practice schedule keeps you focused on the task at hand, and prevents you from mindlessly hitting balls and wasting time.

How does that translate for the average player? If you can commit to one practice session a week, that session doesn't even have to be longer than what you would normally do when you go run through a bucket of balls at the range.

Take that 45 minutes or an hour of time and break it into two halves. Spend one half working on one thing with your full swing practice station, and then go do the same thing with either short game or putting. Set up either the towel ladder we're going to talk about in Chapter 4, or build a putting station that helps you monitor your distance control.

That kind of directed, intentional practice is the quickest way to lower scores.

TO BUILD A PRACTICE STATION,
STRETCH OUT A ROPE ALONG THE TARGET LINE AND
FIX IT TO THE GROUND WITH TWO NAILS.

USE AN ALIGNMENT STICK OR CLUB SHAFT
PERPENDICULAR TO THE TARGET LINE ROPE TO MARK THE BALL POSITION
FOR THE SHOT YOU'RE TRYING TO HIT.

3

BREAKING 80

"No machine is going to tell you why your student isn't breaking 90 or 80. That's teaching. That's why you go on the course with them." — *Brady Riggs*

I f you've seen an issue of Golf Magazine in the last ten years, you know who Brady Riggs is. A Top 100 Teacher for them, he does a lot of instruction articles and swing analysis—and for good reason. Brady has a strong background in science, but he's also an expert at applying the science to the student.

Brady and I met a few years ago at one of Golf Magazine's instruction summits, and he graciously agreed to be a guest on the Dewsweepers. After we talked a few times on the radio, we met up and spent some time together when the NCAA tournament was at Riviera— near Brady's base at Woodley Lakes. I knew that Brady worked with a lot of the players at Cal, and I was teaching some players from Alabama, and we got to talking about our philosophies about developing players.

We became instant great friends.

It's terrific to spend time with Brady because he immediately puts you at ease. He's a casual guy, like I am, and you're likely to see him walking around in a hoodie and shorts. And to him, there's no such thing as a dumb question if it's coming from a sincere desire to learn.

That's so important, not just for a student, but for a teacher as well.

I didn't have the same science background Brady has, and one of the things I struggled with as an up-and-coming teacher was the idea that I'd look foolish asking questions that might be considered basic by other teachers.

But for me, asking questions is the best way to learn, and linking up with Brady and hearing what he has to say about the golf swing has been incredibly helpful. He's a great resource, and he showed me that even if I didn't understand a science-heavy presentation, I was still teaching my players things that were fundamentally correct.

It's a pleasure to talk to Brady about golf instruction because his goal is the same as mine. He wants to take his players from point A to point B and help them solve the most important problems in their games. Science and tools like TrackMan can be a great help, but they won't automatically solve those problems if you don't know how to use them.

They also won't hit the shots for you when you're out on the course.

Brady has one of the best understandings of physics, kinematics and all the science involved in swinging the golf club of any teacher out there, yet his teaching tee isn't some high tech training lab. It's a public range at a place with real grass.

To me Brady is the perfect blend between old school and new school. He understands the art of teaching, playing and coaching, and he also knows the value of technology and how it can help us make people better faster. He also spends a lot of his time working with his players on the course, teaching them how to manage situations and make good decisions.

It's something that's an important part of my teaching plan, as well. Putting somebody on TrackMan is fine, but you can make a huge change in a player's handicap if you show them how to keep track of their mistakes on the course and make better decisions.

One of the neat things about having Brady as a guest is that it's two teachers discussing and exchanging ideas about how to make players better—not an interview where one person is trying to sound smart, or like they have some mysterious key to breaking 80 or 90.

In fact, Brady and I will often text each other afterward and say. "That was good...I think I may use some of that in my teaching." I thought one of the best interviews I have done was when Brady and I sat and answered an email question about how to help two different golfers break 90 and 80 respectively. The answers were different than we might have scripted—but they were the real nitty gritty of how players get better.

I started the conversation with a simple easy to use stat that I learned by good friend and golf statistician Peter Sanders. Peter gave me a basic way to help the average golfer find out where mistakes and errors occur in their game—something pros get from the comprehensive stats the tour keeps.

I have my players keep track of every hole on their scorecard where they've made a double bogey or higher, and mark down what caused that shot—say, a driver out of play, a bladed chip, or whatever the case may be. For example, if you're trying to break 80, you need to be able to understand why you're making any score worse than bogey. If you go out and track your next three rounds religiously, and mark on the scorecard the reason for your double, you'll probably see a pattern. Was it a penalty shot? Bad tee shot? Short game problems? Missing greens in impossible places?

Once you go through that scorecard exercise, you're mapping the process for improvement. Maybe it means you need to work on your driver. Or you need to change some clubs in your bag so you have the right hybrid to hit onto the long par-3s at your course. Maybe you're going for shots you shouldn't on a just-barely-reachable par-5. Or it could well be a mental thing—getting to the

16th tee 4 or 5-over and falling apart coming in because you know the stakes.

The mechanical things are issues you can take to your instructor for time at the range. To go after the decision-making piece, play a practice round with your teacher or one of the best players at the club and ask plenty of questions about strategy and places to miss on given holes.

One of the reasons I run my programs the way I do is because as an assistant, I'd see these great players getting lots of range instruction. But a lot of times, it wouldn't translate into lower scores.

I realized that getting people to play better is far more than dispensing good information. It's helping people learn for themselves what they need to do to play better.

If you really want to get better, one of the best things you can do is play with somebody better and watch what they do. It's the main reason we ask our successful players to come back and spend time with the juniors who are in the program now. Guys like Bobby Wyatt, Robby Shelton, Wilson McDonald, Sam Love, Lee Williams, Smylie Kaufman and Nolan Henke have been so great at spending time with other golfers who want to learn to play better golf.

They're giving the younger players a crash course on how to *play*, not how to *swing*.

Being more prepared in terms of your golf swing and decision making is bound to make you feel more confident when you play. But things aren't always going go perfectly. One of my longest-running guests has to be Dr. Travis Fox. Doc is a wonderful golf psychologist who created the "Beat the Bogeyman" series during the first days of the Dewsweepers. He's been a regular guest and friend ever since.

Doc insists that you have to practice the mental game just like you do the physical side and your swing. I can hear his words right now: "You play golf not work golf," "How's that try working for you?" and "You only play golf for 45 mins in a round the rest of the time you spend talking or beating yourself up." It has changed the way I approach my students both on and off the course.

Two ways we do it are to work on mental routine and to go through experiences that "preview success."

A mental routine is just what it sounds like. You need to have a process you follow on every shot you hit that gets you focused on that process instead of the outcome. It's something you need to practice at the range, so you can take it with you when you play—not something you just start doing when you get to a tournament round.

When you practice your full routine and change clubs and targets the way you would on the course, you're replicating what you're going to see when it's real. It will make you more comfortable when you add the stress of competing. You want to be fully into the idea of hitting that 8-iron and the steps it takes to do that instead of what the ramifications are when you do hit it—whether they're good or bad. If you're standing over the ball thinking that you don't want it to go in the hazard right of the green or that you need to get it close because you've never broken 80, you're going to struggle.

I also am a big believer in helping golfers become more comfortable shooting lower scores. I think learning to be comfortable in the 60s, 70s, 80s, 90s — or whatever your skill level — is has a lot to do with improving your performance when given the opportunity to shoot a great round. That's why I think "previewing success" is so valuable.

Instead of hitting balls one day, get a cart and go play

nine holes at your course by yourself, but do it from the most forward set of tees. Have fun bombing the driver down to places you don't normally get to, and hitting short irons into every hole. Start making some lower scores on holes that normally give you trouble and you'll begin to feel a lot more confident—even if it's on a sub-conscious level.

Does it mean that you'll automatically birdie that 490-yard par-4 when you play it from the back tees next time? No, but you've taken just a little of the intimidating edge off. Also the next time you are even par through 8 holes you wont feel as though you've never been there before either.

Plus, when you do get to lower numbers for real, from your tees, you're going to have some experience on what it feels like. My junior players might go out and smoke nine holes from 2,800 yards and shoot three or four under, which makes them less likely to panic when they get there from 3,600 yards. The same holds true for you no matter what combination of yardage and scoring barrier.

WORKING ON IMPROVING YOUR IMPACT CONDITIONS WITH TRACKMAN
IS GREAT, BUT THE MECHANICS OF THE SWING ARE ONLY ONE PIECE OF THE PUZZLE.
YOU NEED TO BE ABLE TO MAKE GOOD DECISIONS ON THE COURSE, TOO.

4

TURN 5 SHOTS INTO 4

"The only way to make a 5 a 4, a 4 a 3 or a 3 a 2 is with a chip and a putt." — Ben Crenshaw

I t's a moment any golf fan paying attention for the last 25 years can remember like it was yesterday.

Ben Crenshaw rolls in a short putt on the 18th hole at Augusta to win his second green jacket, and bends over, holding his face in his hands and crying.

He wasn't the only one with tears. I was in my little apartment in Birmingham, Alabama, crying like a little girl right along with him when that putt went in.

Crenshaw had been my idol since I was 10 years old—both because of how he played and for his obvious love and passion for the game. One of my all-time thrills in the game came when I was a freshman in college, and I got my picture taken with Ben before a practice round at the Texas Open. I have that picture blown up and framed, hanging in my office.

As I walked along outside the ropes at Oak Hills Country Club in San Antonio, following Ben's every shot, I was amazed by what I was seeing. He had that familiar long, lashing swing, and he was hitting the ball all over the place off the tee. That day on the front nine, he only hit a few greens, but chipped in once and birdied one of the holes where he hit the green and ended up shooting something like two under. He beat the other two guys he played with, and they had hit significantly more greens and fairways.

It was an amazing display of short game from a player who is obviously famous for his skill in that area.

Some 25 years later, I was doing my radio show in Destin when the Champions Tour came to town. Ben was gracious enough to come in and do a live interview with me for the show.

That 20 minutes of radio just reinforced everything I ever believed about him. You won't find a more gracious, natural person in the game of golf. He talked to me like I was an old friend, and gave wonderful, thoughtful answers both about his own game and the game in general.

Near the end of our time together, I asked Ben if there was one lesson or piece of information he would relay to a junior golfer or a beginner that he had learned from his longtime teacher Harvey Penick.

He paused for a minute, thinking, and he said something that truly inspired the way I teach to this day.

"The only way you can make 5 into a 4, a 4 into a 3 or a 3 into a 2 is to learn how to use your wedge and putter," Ben said.

It doesn't matter if I'm teaching one of the members at the Country Club of Mobile or Lee Williams as he's getting ready to go out to a PGA Tour event. We devote at least a third of our time to short game practice—and all of that practice is organized and intentional.

What exactly does "organized" and "intentional" mean?

It means you're never practicing wedges or pitch shots to targets when you don't know the exact distance of those targets.

Technique is obviously a part of the wedge game (and putting), but a majority of good wedge play comes from adding lots and lots of information to your working database.

You can watch me (or Ben or Lee) hit a 68-yard wedge shot, but what exactly does that feel like? What does it feel like on a cold day, when the wind is in your face? How does the ball respond when you're playing on a hot day, on greens that are super firm?

The only way to find out is to find out.

One of the baseline drills I use with all of my students is to set a series of towels out on the range at 40, 50 and 60 yards away, and have players hit all of their wedges to each of those targets. You might hit an almost-full shot with a 60-degree wedge to that 60-yard target, but what does the equivalent shot feel like with your 56-, 52- or 48-degree wedge?

Why is that important to know?

Because the best players understand the mechanics of the shot they need, and then pick the best trajectory to suit the shot at hand. Too many golfers of all skill levels try and force a square peg into a round hole. And by that I mean if they hit their 56-degree sand wedge 90 yards they hit that club from 90 yards whether the trajectory or the spin created by that club is the right fit for that particular shot.

I had a few of my tour pro students out with me, and a group of juniors came over to watch us practicing. We had targets set out at 100, 80 and 60 yards, and I asked the junior players what club they'd hit to that 100-yard target.

After a few seconds of thought, they all said they'd hit a full sand wedge. After all, if you looked at an imaginary yardage card for their set, the SW would have "100" next to it as a maximum comfortable distance.

But when I asked my tour guys the same question, they immediately had a bunch more questions for me. What is the wind doing? How much room do I have in front or behind the flag? The consensus for them was that they'd hit a gap wedge or an easy pitching wedge, because they could flight the ball lower and take the wind more out of play.

The players in the junior group were all very good—boys who could take it under par in a tournament round—but they were shocked by that information. Like most players, they were all very familiar with the "max" yardages for all of their irons, but they got far less comfortable with off-speed, partial shots.

I teach my players to change distances and trajectories in three ways. You can change the size of the pivot, by making your back swing longer or shorter. You can change the speed of your pivot make it faster or slower. Or you can change the length of the lever you're using to hit the ball by either choking up or down on the club.

When a player of any skill levels practices these different variables and hits to real targets with real distances, he or she is giving himself or herself way more options. If you add the ability to do this you won't have to fit a shot into the hole that doesn't fit.

I'm not suggesting that the average 15-handicapper doesn't have anything in his or her swing mechanics that should be improved. But I will say that you will get way, way better if you don't do anything with your mechanics and just go out and practice a bunch of shots from 40 to 100 yards and experiment changing up the clubs you use and trajectories you pick.

Champions Tour player Nolan Henke is a good friend, and he's had a long, productive professional career. He won three times on the PGA Tour in the 1990s, and finished in the top 10 in a handful of majors. He knows what he's talking about.

Nolan told me a great story that I relay to every person I teach who is interested in playing better golf.

When Nolan first went out on tour, in 1988, he was feeling pretty good about himself. He had been a three-time All-American at Florida State, and won seven tournaments in college. But one his caddies immediately told him that he was terrible wedge player—at least in comparison to the guys who were making their living at the game.

So Nolan went out and did a version of the towel setup I was just talking about, setting them out there from 50 to 100 yards and hitting thousands of wedge shots to those distances.

Regardless of your handicap and skill level and regardless of how much time you can practice, if you make this drill your first priority—ahead of blasting drivers and hybrids—you will shoot better scores even if you never take another lesson.

"Within three tournaments, I was getting pretty good at hitting the towels," Nolan said. "And my results showed it. Hitting your long irons better is great, but how many 5-irons are you going to have in a tournament? Compare that to the number of wedges you're going to hit.

"Wedges are a constant."

TECHNIQUE IS IMPORTANT, BUT YOU'LL CUT MULTIPLE STROKES FROM
YOUR HANDICAP IF ALL YOU DO IS PRACTICE HITTING WEDGES TO A GROUP OF TOWELS
SET AT SPECIFIC YARDAGES FROM 40 TO 100 YARDS AWAY.

5

USE ALL THE TOOLS
IN THE TOOL BOX

*"You need to add more tools to your tool box so you can
teach every player what they need." — Mike Adams*

After about a dozen years of full-time teaching, I had gotten to the point where I felt like I was saying a lot of the same things over and over again. My students were improving, but I didn't feel like I was improving as an instructor. I started going to as many teaching seminars and instruction summits as I could, with the hope that I could find some more tools to use with my students.

That's when I heard Mike Adams speak for the first time.

Anybody who has spent more than five minutes in the teaching business knows Mike. He's been recognized on every Golf Digest and Golf Magazine top teacher list since each list was inaugurated, and he revolutionized golf instruction with his LAWS of Golf program, which breaks down teaching approaches by a player's body and swing type. It's always impressive to hear about the number of tour players a given teacher has worked with, and Mike has taught plenty—like Mark Brooks, Bob Estes, Betsy King and Rosie Jones. But Mike's record as a mentor is even more impressive. Dozens of teachers who have worked under Mike have gone on to successful teaching careers, including PGA and LPGA National Teachers of the Year Mike Bender, Mike McGetrick and Krista Dunton.

When I heard Mike talk, he sounded like a mad scientist. He encouraged everybody in the audience not to just take automatically accept what they'd always heard in golf instruction, but to study and experiment and try new things.

It was exciting to hear, and I was even more excited when Mike responded to my phone call after the presentation. He came on the radio with me, and he invited me to come to one of his teaching seminars on Bio-Swing Dynamics out at Pebble Beach.

Mike works out of the fabulous Hamilton Farm Golf Club in Gladstone, New Jersey, in the summer and down at the Medalist Club in Jupiter, Florida—where I went and spent a day and watched him teach a friend and student of mine. It was incredible to spend the day asking questions and bouncing information off a legendary instructor.

Mike really took me under his wing, and opened up an entire new teaching world to me. He showed me how there are many approaches to the same problem, and you owe it to your students and yourself to arm yourself with as many tools to handle those approaches as you can.

After one visit, he told me one of the most flattering—and helpful—things I've heard in all my years teaching. "Tony you already are a great teacher. Just look at the all the people you've helped," he said. "You need to keep learning and learn more tools so that you can help everyone that comes to you. What do you do if you have a student come to you and he can't make much of a turn? You can't just tell him sorry and send him on his way."

Like every teacher, I had built my career around some philosophies and techniques that I liked to use, and I'd really try to get most of my students straightened out with those techniques. But through Mike, I really understood what is obvious when you think about it. People are built differently, and they move differently. You need to be able to build a golf swing that suits what each student is able to do—and tailor it to what they do well naturally.

Mike has pioneered the use of physical testing to really get to the heart of what players can and can't do. He showed me how to do some simple-but-comprehensive evaluations that allow the teacher and student to go down a path that has the most chance of success.

If you really want to get better, I think you need to have a plan and a commitment to the process to make you better—as we talked about earlier.

Without a doubt, part of that plan is having someone around you who can evaluate you physically, to make sure you can do what the teacher wants you to do. Plenty of great programs like TPI certify teachers for their ability to help you in this way, and they're a great resource. If you try to make swings that you physically can't make, you're just setting yourself and your teacher up for failure.

Nobody is as familiar with the technology side of teaching as Mike is, but spending time with him reinforced what I already believed. Technology like Bodi-Trak, Swing Catalyst and TrackMan is extremely valuable, and I use all of it. But it has to validate what you've been teaching—not provide the substance of the teaching itself. I believe the biggest asset of technology is that it gives instructors a way to measure and quantify what is going on. In this way it allows us to measure if we are getting a student better. There's no more of that "Hey, you're hitting is a lot harder now!" stuff. We can measure it, and we can prove if it's true or not!

After the NCAA regionals, I took Robby Shelton over to one of TaylorMade's super-advanced Matlab measuring devices at Greystone Golf Club in Birmingham, Ala., where they have a sophisticated 3D measurement system called Matlab. Robbie's miss was a shot that went to the right, and the Matlab was able to show him that his weight was going into his toes on the downswing.

Great information? Sure, but as a player, you have to be able to understand the context of that information, and know how important it is relative to other pieces of information.

What does that mean in practical terms? Even if you have access to some cool equipment, you don't need to be in front of a TrackMan for every lesson, or constantly measuring yourself on BodiTrack. I know that might be hard for some players to hear—especially the meticulous "engineering" types who feel like there's no such thing as too much information.

But there is!

It's all about merging the use of science and information into your success plan. For example, if one of my students tends to swing too much in-to-out and comes to me just striping his irons, we can measure what he's doing. If his path is 2 degrees to the left, we know that's a pretty good measurement of where he needs ot be when he's playing well.

We'll then save that information for when he's struggling, and we'll go do some checks. We can use Swing Catalyst or BodiTrak to see what is happening with his center of gravity.

The science gives a basis for comparison, which we'll then take out to the range and course and translate into real golf.

It's good to know measurements and trends, but constantly monitoring the numbers takes away from the feel and experience of translating shots into the real game. Sure, you zeroed out your numbers on Track-Man. But how does that translate to the uphill 7-iron you have to hit into the green on the fourth hole at your course?

An effective improvement plan has checkpoints in place—from handicap to TrackMan numbers—interspersed with block practice and on-course work. Block practice means you're identifying one skill to work on—say, improving your pivot—and hitting practice balls specifically to tune that one skill. In that case, it matters in the big picture where the ball goes, but where each individual ball goes isn't as big of a deal. You're looking for trends and improvement.

Once you validate your skill improvement—and TrackMan or BodiTrack are great for that validation—it's time to go out on the golf course and put the improvements into practice. If you're a driving range hero who can't get it done when the wind is blowing and the lie isn't perfect, what have you really accomplished?

The more tools you have at your disposal—whether it's reading ball flight, understanding TrackMan numbers or understanding the marks on the face of your driver—the more equipped you are to not only improve overall, but diagnose the issues in your game as they're happening, out on the course. When you can do something about it!

WHEN YOU'RE WORKING ON YOUR GAME, YOU NEED EVERY TOOL AT YOUR DISPOSAL—
VIDEO, TRACKMAN, ON-COURSE WORK. RELYING ON ANY OF THEM
TO THE EXCLUSION OF THE OTHERS WILL MAKE YOU A ONE-DIMENSIONAL PLAYER.

6

THE HANDS HOLD, THE ARMS CONNECT AND THE BODY DELIVERS THE CLUB

"What do the hands do? Nothing." — *Tom Ness*

When you're just starting out in your profession—whether it's teaching golf or working as a accountant or anything else—you remember when you get your first *real* assignment.

For me, in teaching, it was when I came along to a junior camp run by Golf Digest 50 Best Teacher Rob Akins in Memphis in 2005. Rob's group of teaching friends is filled with the best in the business—Randy Smith, Mark Wood, Hank Johnson, Tom Ness—and those guys were there to support Rob and help some kids really improve their games.

One of the cool things Rob did with his event was encourage each teacher to bring along one of his assistants, and then those assistants would trade around and work with different teachers during the camp so they could get some exposure to some different instruction approaches.

I was working for Hank Johnson at the time, and I was grateful to be invited to come along and work Rob's camp. My assignment for the two days was to work under Tom Ness—another Golf Digest 50 Best Teacher and one of the most well-respected instructors in the game. Tom came up through the ranks at the Golf Digest Schools, working with Bob Toski, Chuck Cook, Davis Love Jr. and Peter Kostis, and he has long been considered one of the sharpest minds in the golf.

He can also come across as intimidating, if you don't

know him, because he always seems to be watching without saying a whole lot.

After I get my assignment, I'm sweating—and honestly hoping we'll be doing putting for the day so I won't get put on the spot and asked something I don't understand.

Sure enough, we're assigned to work with juniors on the full swing, and on the 100-yard walk to the practice tee, Tom doesn't say anything until we're near the end.

"You nervous?" he asks.

I nod, and we get to the first kid on the tee line.

Tom and I watch him hit five or ten balls, and Tom turns his head so that only I can hear.

"What would you do with this kid?" he asks.

I'm sweating, trying to figure out how to answer in a way that doesn't make me look like a complete rookie, and I can't get the words out.

Tom gives me a nudge with his elbow, and says "Relax. This kid sucks. Let's move on to the next one. We're just here to learn something and have some fun."

I let out a long breath and laughed.

Since that day, Tom and I have been great friends, and he's been an incredible sounding board for me. He truly is a walking encyclopedia of the golf swing. I can send him videos of my players and he has a terrific eye, and we've spent hours talking about the swing. We've taught together here in Mobile, and I stayed as a guest at Tom's home in Atlanta....As it was going on, he said almost under his breath, that he had watched one of my students that day out on the course, and his best shots came when he hit a cut, because he was getting more on top of the ball.

His mind is always working.

On one of Tom's appearances on the Dewsweepers, we got an email from a listener who wanted to know about hands are supposed to do during the swing. Tom's answer might have been the shortest one in the history of radio.

"Nothing."

I waited a few beats to let him expand on that, but he stuck with that answer—which might not have made for the best radio, but it emphasized an important point that gets lost on many, many average players.

So many people try to square the clubface with their hands through impact, or move their arms and hands in an effort to apply or create force or to change the plane of the swing. But the quickest way to get better is to start with what Tom has taught me as the bedrock of the swing.

The hands hold on.

The arms connect.

The body delivers the club.

If you can teach players to make a good pivot—winding the upper body and turning through the ball on a steady post—they can start to control the motion of the swing with the big muscles in the body. You immediately feel the club going through impact not because of what you're doing with your arms and hands, but because of what the body is doing.

Terms like "pivot" and "transfer" might be lost on a beginning or struggling player, but it's pretty easy to get anybody to feel the right body motion. You can do it in four or five swings with the drill Tom (and a bunch of other teachers) learned from legendary California instructor Ben Doyle.

Get in a practice bunker and draw a line perpendicular to the target. Set up so line is just inside your lead heel. Make some practice swings contacting the sand in front of that line, and making sure to finish so your chest is in front of it as well.

Sounds easy, right?

Most 20-handicappers make the first swing and can't believe how different it feels to make the divot and pivot in such a different place. They're convinced they would miss the ball if they did it for real.

It's because they've spent so many years either following terrible swing advice like "keep your head down," or they've been hanging back trying to lift the ball in the air all their golfing lives. Their sternum never gets beyond their back leg during the downswing.

As soon as you make a real pivot, put the bottom of the swing in the right place and get your chest past that line, the ball immediately starts coming out with authority— both from the fairway bunker and from a grass lie.

It's the first step toward building real control over your body and the club.

BEN DOYLE'S CLASSIC PIVOT DRILL WILL HELP ANY PLAYER
MAKE MORE SOLID CONTACT. MAKE A LINE IN THE SAND PERPENDICULAR
TO THE TARGET AND SET UP WITH IT INSIDE YOUR LEAD FOOT.

WHEN YOU SWING, MAKE SURE TO MAKE CONTACT WITH THE SAND ON
THE TARGET SIDE OF THE LINE, AND FINISH WITH YOUR CHEST PAST THE LINE AS WELL.
THE ONLY WAY TO DO IT IS TO MAKE A GOOD PIVOT WITH THE UPPER BODY.

7

FUNDAMENTALS ARE FOREVER

"Nobody wants to take the time to put their hands on there correctly. But none of the other stuff matters until that happens." — *Wayne Flint*

When I was coming to the end of my college golf career, my coach had moved to Japan, and I was looking for somebody to help me. I was in the middle of that transition where you're trying to figure out if you're going to be able to play for a living, or you're going to move on to a different job in the golf business.

Back in Birmingham, I heard that Wayne Flint was teaching lots of players on the Auburn golf team and from around the Southeast—guys like Jason Dufner and Brian Gay. I asked around about Wayne, and everybody I talked to said he was a great teacher.

So I went out to Chace Lake Country Club (which is now a shopping mall!) and took a couple of lessons, to see what Wayne was all about. I was a broke college student, and after my second lesson, I wrote Wayne a check for $60. Later on that day, I went out and bought some beer, and my check for the lesson bounced.

Wayne could easily have been done with me then, but he understood, and went on to become a great mentor to me. He sat me down at our first lesson and drew out on a piece of paper the exact fundamentals that were necessary to control the ball and the club.

About halfway through that process, I can distinctly remember thinking, "When am I going to hit a damn ball?" But Wayne kept at it. He explained the importance of the grip and its relation to the clubface. He moved on to talk about the pivot—how it worked and how it functioned as them motor of the golf swing. Next, he covered swing plane, and how the body delivered a lagging clubhead.

It was the first time anybody had laid it all out in front of me that way—and it became the foundation of both what I did in my own swing and how I would teach.

When I eventually decided to go into teaching, he sat me down and explained once again the importance of sticking to these fundamentals, and how sticking to them would guarantee that I made people better.

Those basics—along with a few others—are going to determine the fundamental thing every player and teacher wants to know. Did the ball do what you expected it to? Did it go where you aimed?

In fact, go back to the very beginning, and think about your grip.

Go over and pick up that sand wedge you have against the wall in your basement or office.

When you made your grip, did you just grab the club and do it as a reflex? The grip seems like a straightforward thing—something that everybody learns when they're just starting out. But I can tell you I do just as much work on grip with tour players as I do with beginners. Wayne always has as saying "whats so wrong with taking the time to put a players damn hands on the club correctly" he is right.

It's not that players like Smylie Kaufman, Lee Williams and Zack Sucher or Sam Love forget what makes up a good grip. They know. But every player has his or her grip drift on them. It moves a little weak, or a little strong. It's something that requires persistent attention. I always say your grip is like a 2 year old you have to contantly keep and eye on them.

The next time you pick up the club, take your left

hand and place it on the grip so that it runs through the base of the fingers—and the heel pad of the left hand sits on top of the club. When you do it that way, it makes it so much easier for the club to hinge the left wrist flat and correctly square the face. You don't have a grip that's actually blocking you from moving the club the right way!

Another way to check it? Take that grip and pre-set your impact position with the back of your lead wrist flat and aimed at the target. Now look at the face. Is it pointed at the target too? Mark Wood always called the grip the GPS for your swing. And it is. If you're not pointed at the target this way, you're going to have to do some things in your swing to manipulate the face to compensate—and you're making golf harder than it has to be.

Once you've set a good grip, it will be easier for your right arm to fold and your left arm to hinge in the backswing. At the top, you'll be able to get into a good set position, with the back of your left wrist flat and the club resting on the muscle at the base of your right thumb.

Is it the most exciting stuff to work on? Nope. Not even close.

But getting it wrong makes it really hard to play well, right from the start.

Call up Amazon.com and you'll find thousands of golf instruction books. You can learn every conceivable movement starting from address all the way through the swing. And that information is great to know, but it's secondary to one important move that makes all the other ones work.

The pivot.

The pivot is what makes the arms and hands deliver the club, and it makes the business of hitting the ball where you aimed it much easier to do.

In basic terms, the pivot is the rotation of the body as your upper body winds up on the backswing over your lower body and then unwinds from the ground up back through the ball. It's how you transfer your weight back in the backswing and through on the downswing. And, to be honest, many, many players either do it wrong or don't do it at all. I firmly believe that the biggest area to improve in every handicap or club level golfer is the pivot. If you improve that, you're going to shoot lower scores.

I don't care if you're a 25 handicapper or a scratch. Take this little test and find out if you're pivoting the right way—and getting the most out of your body motion. Pick a 7-iron and hit a practice shot at about three-quarter speed, with a friend taking video of your swing from face-on—right across from you.

When you get to impact, are the buttons on your shirt on top of the ball at impact and finishing over your lead foot? Or are they like most struggling golfers are the buttons getting to the ball on the down swing and then stopping and or going up or backwards as the club passes and goes through the ball.

If you struggle with a slice or some other kind of weak contact, I'll be anything those buttons never go through the ball to get to your lead foot? If you hook it, those buttons hang back behind the ball and the clubhead passes and the face shuts through impact.

Forget about controlling individual parts of your body and work on making three-quarter swings so that those buttons end up in line with your lead foot and you'll dramatically improve your pivot—and gain way more control over where your ball goes.

When it comes to swing plane, it's more important to understand what it is than to necessarily try to conform your plane to somebody else's. If you're starting from scratch, it will make the game easier if you swing the club on the same relative plane throughout—but that doesn't mean that I'd go and change Matt Kuchar's swing to a more upright plane.

What does "plane" mean? I still use the same definition Wayne gave me all those years ago. The ball sits on an imaginary target line that points where you want the ball to go. The club swings so that one end of the club or the other is pointing at an extension of the target line.

If your swing plane is too upright, it means that an imaginary line coming from the butt or clubhead end would extend and hit the ground in between you and the ball. If your plane is too flat, the line would extend past the ball, over in front of you somewhere.

You can monitor your swing plane easily with smart phone video, mostly to get a sense for how consistent your plane is. A super upright plane will make it easier to hit your short irons, but will give you more problems with longer clubs. The opposite is true with a flatter plane. As I said before, there's an "ideal" swing plane, but it's more important to have a consistent plane that works for the shots you're trying to hit.

There's a reason Wayne gave me those basics to start teaching all those years ago. He knows what will make most players better. He's probably the most underrated really great teacher in the game.

Try these fundamentals of grip, pivot, plane and impact and you'll understand why I've modeled a lot of my developmental teaching material after what Wayne does.

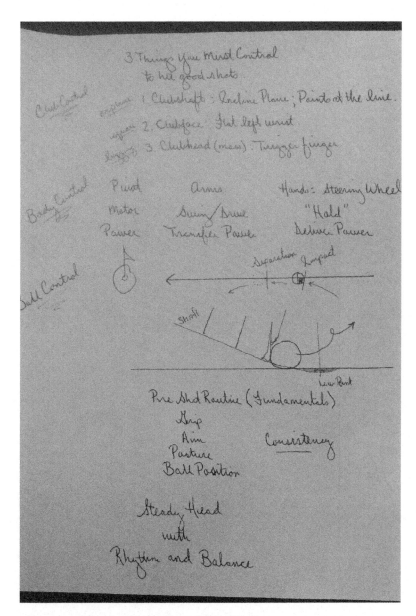

HERE YOU CAN SEE WHAT ONE OF WAYNE'S FIRST LESSONS
LOOKS LIKE MAPPED OUT. IT'S BROKEN DOWN INTO THREE SIMPLE
CATEGORIES—CLUB CONTROL, BODY CONTROL AND BALL CONTROL.

WAYNE STARTS HIS FIRST LESSON WITH A STUDENT THE SAME WAY
WHETHER THEY'RE A BEGINNER OR AN ALL-AMERICAN. EVERYBODY NEEDS
TO KNOW HOW TO BUT THEIR HANDS ON THE CLUB.

8

ARE YOU GETTING BETTER?

"If you really want to get better,
go to someone who at some point has actually made
someone very good." — Tony Ruggiero

'm really lucky. I get to do a job I love every day, helping players get better. And on the side, I get to spend time talking to some of the most interesting people in the world of golf on the radio.

But in both of those jobs, I talk to players who are frustrated with this game. They're putting in the time and effort, but they aren't getting better. Or they've improved for a while but have gotten to the point where that improvement has stalled.

Where are you with your game?

Are you happy with the way you're playing?

We all want to get better, but do you see a way for it to happen for you?

In this book, we've talked about some of the simple mechanical and inspirational things some of my favorite golf people have said about the swing and the game— and I hope those things will help you as much as they've helped me.

But what if you're still stalled?

It's something that's easy for a tour player to see, right away. He looks at tournament finishes, the money list and statistical breakdowns to get a handle on what exactly he needs to do.

If you're serious about getting better, you need to do the same thing.

You have a handicap number (official or otherwise). You need to make a goal of where you want that number to be at the end of the season. When I'm working with a student who is committed to that process of improvement, our most common goal is to cut 20 percent of that handicap number in one year.

That means one shot for a 4-handicapper, or four shots for 20-handicapper.

Is that an ambitious goal?

Sure.

Is it possible?

Absolutely.

You need to make that instruction plan we've been talking about throughout this book. It's time to work with an instructor to figure out what your weaknesses are, and what the plan is to attack those weaknesses.

Bryan Gathright shared a great story with me on the radio. He talked about how he used a ladder approach with some of the players he has taught, like Jimmy Walker and Notah Begay. Bryan would sit down with the player and rank playing attributes from strongest to weakest on a ladder.

It's a great exercise for you to try for yourself.

On the top rung of the ladder, write down the strongest part of your game—putting, driving, short irons, mental game, whatever it is. The bottom rung is the weakest part of your game. The plan for the year is to maintain the strength of the top rung, but figure out why the bottom rung is the weakest and address it.

Do you have a mechanical issue? A technique issue? An equipment issue? Is it because of a lack of focus, or a faulty practice plan?

This simple approach can help anybody get off a plateau and trend in the right direction. If you aren't having conversations like this with your teacher, it means your teacher doesn't have that kind of plan for you, either.

Next, go out and build yourself a set of basic statistics. How many fairways and greens are you hitting? How many putts are you taking? When you miss fairways and greens, where is your predominant miss? How far to you hit each of your clubs on average? How many short game mistakes to you make in a given round?

It's so much easier to get that information now than it ever has been. Systems like GameGolf and Shot-By-Shot hook up to your clubs and send all of the information to your smartphone. There's no excuse not to know in general terms what you do and don't do on the golf course.

If you don't keep track of your tendencies and make a plan to address them, you're just going out and hitting balls. I say all you are doing is getting better at not being any good.

Making the plan and committing to it are two huge steps, and if you've done that, I give you a tremendous amount of credit. You've gone farther than a lot of players.

Don't stop now.

As you work your way through your plan, keep track of your game and make sure that your skills are improving and those improvements are actually causing your scores to go down.

This is where a lot of players with good intentions get stuck. They take lots of lessons and put in the effort to get better, but the effort doesn't produce lower scores.

If you're working on your putting, but you aren't taking fewer putts, why is that?

The answer might be simple—you're hitting more greens, but are farther from hole. Or it might be more complex—the stuff you're working on in your putting isn't working for you.

There's no shame in adjusting and changing your plan if it isn't producing the results you want. My goal here in this book is the same as it is if you came to see me in Mobile or in Panama City Beach. I want to give you things that will get you hitting the ball better both today and in the long term, but also give you the information you need to make more informed decisions about your swing and your game.

I want to teach you how to coach yourself...and have some fun while you do it! I firmly believe that most people want to get better but just don't know how.

You need to have a plan and you need to have a way of monitoring yourself to make sure you are really doing what you are trying to do. Take advantage of all the smartphone technology out there to record your swing on Swing Catalyst or V1.

When you understand the bullet points on your notecard and what you need to work on, you can monitor yourself on video to make sure you're on track. You don't have to wait two or three weeks until you see your teacher again. You are always moving forward and you are always measuring and monitoring to make sure you are moving forward.

If you're stuck and aren't sure what to do with your game, go to my DewsweepersGolf.com and send me an email, or come down and see me on the lesson tee. Or you can become an honorary Dewsweeper by catching the show on PGA Tour Radio.

Thank you for spending some time with me.

WALKING WITH MY FRIEND AND STUDENT SMYLIE KAUFMAN AT THE 2014 U.S. OPEN AT
PINEHURST. HE MISSED THE CUT, BUT HE IMPROVED STEADILY AND WON HIS FIRST PGA
TOUR EVENT AT THE 2016 SHRINERS HOSPITAL FOR CHILDREN OPEN IN LAS VEGAS.

BOBBY WYATT WAS ONE OF MY FIRST PROMINENT STUDENTS. HE LED ALABAMA TO AN NCAA TITLE IN 2013, AND THIS PICTURE WAS TAKEN RIGHT AFTER BOBBY HELPED THE AMERICAN TEAM WIN THE WALKER CUP AT NATIONAL GOLF LINKS LATER THAT SAME SUMMER.

ACKNOWLEDGEMENTS

One of the most memorable pieces of advice I got at the beginning of my teaching career was a question.

Do you want to be a good teacher, or do you want to be a great teacher? The path to being great is much more difficult.

Truer words could not have been spoken.

I wouldn't call myself a great teacher, but my drive and passion has always been to get there—and the journey would not have been even remotely possible without the help of a lot of people.

Yvonne and Breen Kelly, you've always been so understanding of the nights away from home, the nights on the road and the constant flood of house guests who stay for a night or two while they work on their games. Your patience and support are truly amazing.

The Ruggiero family—my parents, Don and Josie, and my sister Alessandra—I'm glad we're able to share so many good times.

Hank Johnson, you gave me my start and a wonderful base of knowledge. You've touched so many of us who want to be teachers. I hope you know how sad it is for me that we don't talk anymore.

Abby Ruggiero, I know I've missed out on a lot of your life during this journey, but I'm so appreciative of your support, and to Mary Abigail and Tripp Hagen for allowing me to be a part of your lives.

Ralph Carroll, I'm grateful for all the hours you've spent listening to me on the radio and making me sound smart. Your vision and advice are priceless. I'm listening, even when it seems like I'm not!

Mark Wood and Wayne Flint, you've been role models for me, but more importantly, you've been great friends. Teaching with you has made all of this so much more meaningful.

St. Mary's University gave me my shot as a player. Rich Dupre, Alex Miller and Kevin Finger, you were the best teammates in the world. My favorite rounds are still the ones with you guys. Buddy Meyer and Jim Zeleznak, you showed me what it means to be a coach, and inspired me to do the same. I still love getting the chance to learn from you.

Michael Heninger, you built my first real teaching home at the Santa Rosa Beach Club, and you gave me the confidence to go out on my own. I miss you every day.

Wade Hamilton, you're the best golf professional and dearest friend I could ever have. You're the only one who truly understands me!

Scott Smith and the staff at the Country Club of Mobile, thank you for being supportive of everything we do. I'm proud to be a part of the team. Thank you as well to the Board of Directors and members. I appreciate the understanding and believe in what we're building at CCM.

Meg McDonald, I wouldn't remotely know what to do with myself without your help every day. I'm grateful.

Dr. Travis Fox, thank you for letting me lay on your couch for ten years. You're a true friend, and I'm a better person for it.

Jeremy Elliott and Mac Barnhardt, you're super-agents who have helped me learn and improve my craft. You've been there for all the good and bad. You're the best support staff and team anybody in the business could have.

Jody Graham and Kemper Sports, you believed in me and gave me the opportunity to bring our instruction program back to the Panhandle. Thank you for that opportunity.

Chip Holcombe, you rolled the dice to offer Cleveland Golf's support to an upstart local teacher and radio guy, and I couldn't have a better partner or friend over all these years. Your support and belief in me has been amazing. Mitch McConnell, you did the same with Buick, and I'm so appreciative of the support.

Thank you to all the great teachers, guests and friends who have spent time with me on the Dewsweepers. To name a few: Brady Riggs, Bryan Gathright, Mike Adams, Tom Patri, Eddie Merrins, Michael Breed, Mark Blackburn, Bhrett McCabe, Carol Preisinger, Jim McLean, Debbie Doniger, Brian Manzella, Nancy Quarcelino, Ted Sheftic and Ed Ibarguen.

Bobby Wyatt, you were the first great player to take a chance on me, and it's been amazing to grow up in the game with you as a friend and student.

I'm grateful to all of my professional and collegiate players for their trust, including: Lee Williams, Sam Love, Zack Sucher, Wilson McDonald, Smylie Kaufman, Hannah Collier, Robby Shelton, Davis Riley, Tom Love-

ACKNOWLEDGEMENTS

lady, Robby Prater, Steven Setterstrom, Ryan Benton, Wesley Hunter and many others who have shared the time and effort we put into this great game.

I owe a huge thank you to Matthew Rudy and Tim Oliver for your work making this book come to life. Matt, you took a crazy idea and showed me more than just how to turn it into chapters. You helped me get more in tune with what I do and believe as a teacher. I never would have believed it was possible. Thank again, and I hope I haven't run you off. I want to do a sequel!

And finally, thank you to all my students and listeners for dedicating their time either on the practice tee or the radio. We still have a long way to go together!

—TONY RUGGIERO / MOBILE, ALA. / DECEMBER 1, 2015

NOTES

NOTES

NOTES

Made in the USA
Monee, IL
10 September 2021